Sparrow Seed:
The Franciscan Poems

by
T.H.S. Wallace

Copyright 2006 by T.H.S. Wallace

First Printing 2007

ISBN 978-0-944350-72-0

Cover Design: Shari Pickett Veach
Book Design and Author Photograph: Donna Gentile Wierzbowski

All rights reserved. No portion of this book may be reproduced, stored in a electronic retrieval system or transmitted in any form or by any means—electronic, mechanical, photocopy, recording or other form—except for brief quotations in printed reviews, without the prior permission of the publisher.

Friends United Press
101 Quaker Hill Drive
Richmond IN 47374
friendspress@fum.org
www.fum.org

Library of Congress Cataloging-in-Publication Data

Wallace, T. H. S. (Terry H. S.)
  Sparrow seed : the Franciscan poems / by T.H.S. Wallace.
    p. cm.
  ISBN 978-0-944350-72-0 (alk. paper)
  1. Francis, of Assisi, Saint, 1182-1226—Poetry. 2. Francis, of Assisi, Saint, 1182-1226—Legends. I. Title.
  BX4700.F6W23 2007
  271'.302—dc22
  [B]
                                                2007008180

*For Phyllis Reynolds Luckenbaugh,
who lived her faith with joy and humor
in the midst of suffering,
and for her husband, Paul,
and daughters, Lisa and Pamela.*

Acknowledgments: The author thanks the following publications for printing versions of the poems contained here in *Sparrow Seed*:

Connecticut Review: *The Day the Door-Gate Fell upon Our Sister Clare, Saint Fraud.*

Inspirit (Winter 2005, Issue #1 and Fall 2005, Issue #2): *Introduction, Cabbage Planting Made Simple, Francis Falls Among Thieves, On the Proper Use of Fox Fur, How Francis Gave Away the New Testament, What Kissing Lepers Is All About.*

Raw on the Bars of Longing (Harrisburg, PA: Rabbit Press, 1994): *Dancing Before Cardinals, Francis Explains What He Does at the Ruined Chapel of San Damiano, Francis Mourns His Father, Francis Proposes to the Lady Clare, How the Poor Point Out Your House.*

The Wildwood Journal (Spring 2004, Volume XXIV): *Francis Explains What It Means To Be Bound and Led in Truth, Saint John the Simple, How We Lost Our Mantles, The One Who Thought Nothing of Money, Another Use for Donkey Dung, Francis and the Rabbit, We Are to Walk Gently, Francis Insults God and His Feathers, Why Francis Begged Meat and Ate Grapes in the Vineyard, Francis and the Body's Poverty,* and *Poverty Clothed by Christ's Mercy.*

*"You see the truth of me,
Fathers, small like my Friars, those
little brown sparrows of men.
God counts them over and over.
He gave them a home in the air,
and their food and their feathers.
They've no pride, just the pleasure
of wings, their dip and glide and slip
on the rippling wind. They're simple
by nature, Fathers. We who aren't
must be simple by grace."*

— *from* Dancing Before Cardinals

Contents

Preface ix

Introduction xi

What Kissing Lepers Is All About 1
What Kissing Lepers Is All About 3
Francis Falls Among Thieves 5
Francis Explains What He Does at the Ruined
    Chapel of San Damiano 6
Francis Mourns His Father 7
The Priest Who Doled Out Penance Only to
    Those Who Could Pay 9
Sparrow Study 11
How Francis Gave Away the New Testament 12
On Sweeping the Temple 13
The One Who Thought Nothing of Money 14
Another Use for Donkey Dung 15
The Tiniest Portion 16
Dancing before Cardinals 18
Not Without Witnesses 20

Cabbage Planting Made Simple 23
Cabbage Planting Made Simple 25
Sparrow Seed 27
Sparrow Feathers 28
Francis Proposes to the Lady Clare 30
Clare by Name and Nature 31
Francis Speaks to His Daughters 34
The Day the Door-Gate Fell Upon Our Sister Clare .. 35
Gubbio Cheese Cake 36
Saint John the Simple 37
Whenever Asked for Prayer 39
The Hungriest Thieving Murderers 40

We Are to Walk Gently 43
We Are to Walk Gently 45
Francis and the Rabbit 46
Francis Insults God and His Feathers 47
How the Poor Point Out Your House 48
Because the House Is Ours, Not Yours 49
Saint Fraud 50
When I Grew Tired of Walking Behind My Brother... 52
Francis Explains What It Means
   to Be Bound and Led in Truth 53

That Winter of His Faithfulness 55
That Winter of His Faithfulness 57
How We Lost Our Mantles 58
Why Francis Begged Meat and Ate Grapes
   in the Vineyard 60
The Man with Murder's Face 62
On the Proper Use of the Fox Fur 64
The Morning Francis Taught Us All to Sing 65
Francis and the Body's Poverty 67
The Little Dog Speaks of the Blind Man 68
Poverty Clothed by Christ's Mercy 71

A Note on the Author 73

Preface

The genesis of *Sparrow Seed* lay in a dream I've had of writing a series of poems similar to that medieval classic *The Little Flowers of St. Francis*. My hope is that some of the poems here come close to the simple charm and grace of those tales. To prepare myself for the effort, I researched most of the extant medieval texts on Francis. My review included his writings and poetry and most of the 13th and 14th century biographies of him. My intent in this research was to come as close as I could to the early Franciscan experience, eschewing the hagiography and centuries of accretions that have overlaid, distorted, and obscured that lively and engaging witness.

My original intent necessarily required me to address several ancillary purposes. Thus, *Sparrow Seed* also attempts to capture the life and spirit of Francis of Assisi and others in, or influenced by, the early Franciscan movement—and to capture that life and spirit in their very voices. It particularly explores their no-nonsense faith and practice, their tough-minded faithfulness, and their all-too-human natures, natures they struggled to control and turn to good works.

I am grateful for the work of several colleagues who encouraged, challenged, and aided in finishing *Sparrow Seed*. Sandrine Simeon, Molly Smith, Leslie Thompson, Vicky Fake, and Gail Varney spent many hours reading and critiquing the entire work and made very helpful suggestions that measurably improved the poems here, and Donna Gentile Wierzbowski's talents in book design and technical preparation were invaluable in preparing the manuscript for press.

    — T.H.S. Wallace, Camp Hill, Pennsylvania
    May 2005

Introduction

Francis of Assisi was born the son of a highly successful merchant and took first to soldiering, before becoming what he himself called "a fool for God." As the latter, he first set his hand to rebuilding small churches and embracing poverty with as great a devotion as most men embrace wealth, becoming by the end of his life one of Christianity's greatest church reformers. Francis' life, vision, and example have been so powerful that they still speak strongly, and disconcertingly, to us in the 21st century. Mark Gilli, in his book *Francis of Assisi and His World*, observes that

> "...the Francis who calls us to peace and respect for creation—causes we readily sign up for—is the same Francis who challenges our age, as he did his own age, by speaking and living against our most vexing sins.
>
> "In a secular age, when talk of God is awkward or rigidly privatized, stands the deeply pious Francis, whose God intoxication drove everything he did. In a materialistic world, where the meaning and measure of life is counted by the things we buy and the experiences we enjoy, the barefoot, raggedly robed Francis calls us to simplicity and poverty. In cultures drowning in rampant individualism, in which we baulk at submitting to anything outside of self, Francis tells us to abandon our lives in complete obedience to something bigger than ourselves.
>
> "In short, Francis would instill in us, as he tried to instill in his contemporaries, profound gratitude and humility—towards God, our world and even the flawed institutions that have

nurtured us. In the end, although our modern world wishes to discard so much of Francis into the rubbish bin of history, it is the medieval Francis who shows the modern world a better way. [182-183]"

Francis was devoid of that dour judgmental attitude so typical of some reformers. Rather, he radiated an irrepressible joy, humor, and humanity that blossomed into both compassion and poetry. As G. K. Chesterton noted, Francis "looked out freshly upon a fresh world that might have been made that morning." His is a vision still worthy of seeking and finding today.

Wealth's Tenor

Francis came into the world in 1182, at the dawn of that period we have come to know as the High Middle Ages, a period his life and ministry helped to transform spiritually, artistically, and emotionally. Francis was born into what today we might term an upper middle class family and to a father, Pietro Bernardone, who aimed to raise his family still further, perhaps into the nobility. A notably successful cloth merchant, he lavished on Francis the funds, the clothing, the parties, and accoutrements that made the young man attractive both to others of his class and to the young and coming noble youths of other local families. When Francis wanted the armor and weaponry needed for knightly military career, Bernardone underwrote them and did so more than once. When his son needed the funds for lavish clothing and parties, the father supplied them without complaint. Travels into France with his father introduced Francis to its culture and the itinerant troubadours that were the popular musicians of the day, musicians that fostered the poet in him. Given nearly everything he wanted, Francis stood at the threshold of manhood with a multiplicity of dreams and possibilities for his life: to be "king of the revels," a knightly adventurer, the most popular young man about town, troubadour, merchant, man of influence and wealth. A man who knew the tenor of wealth and might indeed be termed *Wealth's Tenor*.

Augustine of Hippo's observation, that the heart "is restless until it finds rest in God," is a truth for all ages. Restless with dreams of glory, Francis joined his fellow townsmen in 1202 in a war against Assisi's neighboring city state and competitor, Perugia. For Assisi, the war was short-lived and disappointing. Perugia defeated and captured many of its opponents, Francis among them, in a battle near the San Giovanni Bridge, and imprisoned them to await reparations in the form of ransom. That ransom was a while in coming and Francis was only released a year later, ill—perhaps with the early tubercular infection that was to take his life 24 years later. Yet, while imprisonment and illness may have dented Francis' dreams, they were not particularly defining moments in his spiritual development.

From Knight to Herald of the Great King

Francis' spiritual life was not the result of a single, overwhelming conversion experience that left him totally changed, but rather a series of key revelations and acts that brought him increasing clarity and direction as to what God's will was for his life. As one early chronicler expressed it, the young Francis was "changed...in mind, not in body...." He had not yet fully entered into new life in Christ Jesus.

He did not immediately abandon his dreams of knightly glory. He rearmed himself for another military campaign in 1205, one brought abruptly to a close in Apulia by a revelatory dream and his giving his armor to a needy older knight. Though Francis' role as "king of the revels" continued for some months, his friends began to notice an alteration in his attitude that suggested momentous inward changes: he was losing interest in the wild partying, being drawn toward someone he called the "most beautiful Lady," Lady Poverty.

His spiritual growth during this period was characterized by a series of fits and starts, interspersed with misinterpretations and missteps. In spite of the latter, God turned them and Francis to His purpose. At first Francis wandered the countryside around Assisi in prayer and meditation, until one day, as he prayed in the ruined chapel of St. Damian, he heard a voice from the crucifix instructing him to "rebuild my church" (see "Francis Explains What He Does at the Ruined Chapel of San Damiano," p. 6). A novice in spiritual ways, Francis took the command literally, rather than figuratively, and set about refurbishing the little sanctuary and repairing the chapel's walls. Another key moment in his spiritual development occurred when he succeeded in overcoming his extreme repugnance toward lepers (see "What Kissing Lepers Is All About," p. 3).

The most momentous of Francis' missteps occurred, when—to underwrite his work at St. Damian—he sold bolts of his father's best cloth and one of his father's finer horses, while Bernardone was out-of-town on a business trip. At best, this youthful indiscretion might be termed a misunderstanding: "what is my father's is mine as his first born;" at worst, it might be termed a "holy theft." Bernardone, himself, did not try to parse which it was. Increasingly mortified and irritated by his son's strange behavior, neglect of business, and disobedience to the paternal will and dreams, Bernardone first beat and tried to imprison Francis at home and, when that failed, brought him up on charges before the bishop of Assisi in order to seek reparation. Francis' action and Bernardone's anger bring one of the most dramatic early scenes in the former's spiritual development, the final disownment of father by son, a scene both must have regretted (see "Francis Mourns His Father," p. 7).

From this moment on, Francis' spiritual growth gathers clarity and momentum.

Dancing before Cardinals

Drawn out of his old ways, Francis began to live out a new life in Christ Jesus, one that would bring great fruit, both to the church and western civilization. Like his initiation into faith, his entry into his ministry and mission is one of a series of steps that led him steadily deeper into the life, the role, and the purpose he was meant to serve. Francis lived and worked at first alone, but not lonely: ridiculed, but not unhappy. He worshiped and spent his time repairing several ruined chapels, following out his initial charge "to rebuild." Though he was rejected by family, pelted with refuse by ignorant neighbors, and even mugged by thieves (see "Francis Falls Among Thieves," p. 5), Francis moved forward, not only undaunted, but with even greater zeal and joy.

His sincerity, his joy, his openness and honesty—his new life—became more and more difficult to ignore and soon began to draw others. The first was a wealthy noble named Bernard, who gave his fortune away and joined Francis. Soon there are others, like the priest Sylvester who faced the truth of his sorry life and found himself drawn towards a new one with Francis (see "The Priest Who Doled Out Penance Only to Those Who Could Pay," p. 9). By 1209, Francis had gathered a small cadre of 12 followers and sought the way of life by which he and his new brothers were supposed to live. The Gospel According to Matthew, he found, spoke directly to their situation:

> *Preach this message: 'The kingdom of heaven is near.' Heal the sick, raise the dead, cleanse those who have leprosy, drive out demons. Freely you have received, freely give. Do not take along any gold or silver or copper in your belts; take no bag for the journey, or extra tunic, or sandals or a staff; for the worker is worth his keep.*

Francis and his brothers were called to a life of radical poverty, living the gospel message with utter faithfulness. They were called to be a stark contrast to the corrupt age in which they lived, exposing its decadent condition. They were to become a moral reformation within the Church of their time, by the very force of their example, preaching, and faithfulness.

Francis recognized immediately that such a radical departure from the degraded standards of the World would draw concern, distress, even hostility, and thus he took his modest band of brothers to Rome to seek the Church's blessing on their endeavor. The importance of this request cannot be overemphasized. Their very appearance had an element of risk and their receipt of any official recognition and acceptance was by no means a foregone conclusion.

The initial tension in the Curia must have been palpable when Francis and his *friars minores* appeared, for the Pope and Curia had seen men like these before, and watched such movements turn sour and become threats to both the Church and the established order. Yet, as Francis spoke, his sincerity, clarity, and honesty—and his remarkable respect and politeness—turned the hearts and minds even of these powerful men, men too well aware of the vagaries of human nature. The scene must have been very close to that portrayed in "Dancing Before Cardinals" in the following pages. In spite of the abortive history of similar movements, it was plain that Francis and his Brothers were not in rebellion against the Church of their time, but sought to draw it into essential faithfulness with the Gospel: something the Pope and many members of the Curia were as concerned about as anyone, for they themselves were all too well aware of, and troubled by, the state of the Church.

Little Brothers, Poor Clares, and More

Observers of Christianity over the last 2,000 years have repeatedly noted that when it is truly lived out, that living witness is overwhelmingly powerful. The presence of true faith is known by its fruits, the fruits of utter fidelity, uncompromising honesty, and daily displays of extraordinary compassion by the most ordinary people.

The appearance of living witnesses to the truth of Christ's gospel often revolutionizes the generation in which it appears and such was the case with Francis and his Brothers. In their decadent and disillusioned world filled with too many corrupt priests, self-seeking prelates, and degraded religious, the opposite now emerged with dramatic results.

When Francis and his Brothers returned from Rome with the Pope's oral blessing on their small brotherhood and its primitive rule, Francis divided the group up by twos and sent them out to preach the gospel. The initial appearance of this apostolate—dressed in rags, dedicated to poverty, and depending on Divine providence and local charity for their existence—at best piqued the curiosity of the people who heard and saw them and at worst piqued people's suspicion and rude rejection. However, the Brothers persevered in their work and witness and the equanimity with which they bore rejection and violence soon began to win hearts and draw people to the gospel.

Within three years (1209-1212) of their appearance, the results were astonishing. Men across Europe were drawn to join the *friars minores*, first by the hundreds and then by the thousands. Francis soon had to establish a second order after drawing a young woman of the nobility, one Clare of the Offreducii family, to join his work. She became Francis' clearest convert, the one who most closely understood him and lived out the life to which he called men and women.

As her example quickly attracted other women—including her sister, Agnes, and then her mother—to this fresh manifestation of the faith, Francis established the Order of the Poor Clares and settled them at the restored chapel of St. Damian. Clare proved as devoted as the Brothers to strict poverty and utter obedience to the gospel (see "Francis Proposes to the Lady Clare," p. 30, and "Clare by Name and Nature," p. 31). Single men and women weren't the only ones responding to the Franciscan call to faithfulness. Married men and women and their families declared interest, leading to yet a Third Order, living out Francis' Rule in their marriage.

Well before the decade was out, thousands of Franciscans were traveling to the annual Pentecost Chapters of the Order outside of Assisi at Portiuncula, the birthplace of the *friars minores*. For Francis, these were years filled with preaching and leading his Brothers, both by example and advice, example and advice that still lives vividly in many of the chronicles and remembrances written by followers after his death.

The Final Years

1219 was a watershed year, both for Francis and his Orders. After several attempts to travel to Muslim lands to preach the gospel and, if need be, experience martyrdom, Francis finally found way opening to travel to Jerusalem and then to Damietta in Palestine to preach to the crusaders there. The medieval chronicles hold nothing concerning his visit to Jerusalem, but what he saw in the crusader camps would have shaken a man less firm in his faith. The crusader violence and decadence Francis witnessed and spoke against, and the lack of inspired military leadership against a brilliant and determined Muslim foe fighting on his own soil, spelled coming disaster. Francis went so far as to prophesy defeat in battle, a prophecy fulfilled by the Muslims' slaughter of 6,000 crusaders. Francis carried his own work forward in his usual startling fashion: he took himself and his message to the enemy, was captured, brought before Sultan Malek-el-Khamil, the remarkable Muslim leader, and challenged him with the gospel. The fact that Francis was allowed to return to the Christian lines is eloquent testimony to the integrity and respect each man had for the other.

Francis' return to Europe in 1219 proved much less auspicious. He arrived ill with a number of physical problems, problems affecting both his eyesight and his general health (tubercular symptoms among them). These he shrugged off as best he could and continued to spread the gospel. However, he soon discovered to his dismay that his Brothers were drifting away from their original witness. At Bologna and Assisi, he could not suppress his anger and vigorously admonished his Brothers to return to the original intent of their Order (see "How the Poor Point Out Your House," p. 48, and "Because the House Is Ours, Not Yours," p. 49). However, within the year, it was plain that Francis no longer had the physical strength to lead his thousands of followers; at their annual Pentecost gathering at Porticuncula, the Order's birth place outside of Assisi, he humbly relinquished his control to the Order's first vicar, Peter of Catania. From this point on Francis knew he could only, and must, lead by example and preaching. He set himself to continue his strict and faithful witness to the end.

The final six years of Francis' life were ones of remarkable witness, in spite of the continuing decline of his health (see, for instance, "The Morning Francis Taught Us All to Sing," p. 65). Though he continued to travel locally on preaching missions, he spent more and more time with a few of his Brothers in prayer and contemplation often in secluded hermitages. The church, as a whole, struggled to institutionalize his massive reform movement, laboring with

Francis and many of his Brothers to develop a revised, and less strict, rule. Both Francis and Clare, to the end of their lives, remained dedicated to the strict primitive rule with which they began their work. However, the church worked to shape a revised rule that would allow for better institutional care, direction, oversight, and discipline of the new Orders. Francis and many of his followers sought a revised rule that continued to emphasize the vision and exceptional strictness of the early brotherhood. Others among his followers, and especially among the order's leadership, sought to ameliorate what they felt were the harshest aspects of the brotherhood's original intent. The result proved hard to come by, with a first revised rule approved at the Pentecost chapter of the brotherhood in 1221, but soon superseded by a second rule approved by both the chapter and the Pope in 1223.

The chroniclers of the early Franciscan movement have left us with many vignettes from Francis' last years, ones that touch on his growing blindness; his suffering from tubercular infections, arthritis, edema, and malnutrition. They detail, not only his great suffering (and the various primitive, painful, and largely unsuccessful treatments he underwent, like the attempt to relieve his eye problems by the application of searing irons to his temples), but also his remarkable faithfulness in spite of it. During this period, when he could do little else, he produced some of his greatest poetry, including his *Canticle to Brother Sun.* Near the end of his days, while on retreat at Mt. Alverna, Francis received the stigmata, the spiritual imprimatur on his faithfulness. With typical modesty, he sought to hide the stigmata wounds to his hands, feet, and side until his death which occurred in October of 1226.

 # WHAT KISSING LEPERS IS ALL ABOUT

What Kissing Lepers Is All About

It is not that I hated them:
I *loathed* them, the sight
and smell and sound of them.

I held my nose, even if they
stood well down wind of me,
and spurred my horse to a greater

distance. I could afford then to ride
wide, moving smartly off, and my
companions never judged me poorly.

But the day I touched my first leper—
he suddenly appeared before me,
like one more stinking ghost haunting

my already too haunted world.
I cursed and shamed him for his
begging, turned and galloped off

at full speed. Then stunned by the leper
I had become, I halted, turned, and knew
what I must do to be saved from myself.

I galloped back, dismounted, and,
as he thrust his fingerless stub of
a hand out to ward away violence,

I palmed him a coin and planted
a kiss on his ruined cheek,
and both he and I stood there

marked by more than surprise.
Mind you: I did not do this by myself,
but was made stronger than myself.

Brothers, we must embrace all the world's bitter, haunted, angry sinners like ourselves, just as Christ embraced us.

This is what kissing lepers is all about.

Francis Falls Among Thieves

Francis simply wandered about
in those first days of his new life
filled with a fresh, unfettered ecstasy,

a half naked fool singing praises
to Christ—in French no less—
and why they assaulted him,

no one knows. Perhaps
they thought him his former self
in disguise and hoped for a rich taking.

Perhaps they were desperately poor thieves,
for Francis always remembered them
with a certain pity and some fondness.

"Who be you, fool!" they thundered.
"The Great King's herald!" he roared,
which earned him only a swift clout

and a pitch into a deep ditch filled
with snow, that left him senseless,
they thought, to come to his senses,

but he bounded out like a happy dog,
shook off the snow, and went on
his way even happier than before.

Francis Explains What He Does at the Ruined Chapel of San Damiano

I sat in the chapel with Christ
bleeding before me, the dark
and animal world restless
beyond its broken walls,
and He told me to mend them.

So I beg stones for my church.
Sometimes I gather but
spittle and scorn, sometimes
more—gristle, the stale ends
of bread. For all of it

I utter God's peace and give
thanks like the fool I am.
I beg stones and cradle
them away like children
and am happy to work till

my soft bones ache. Then
I go in to rest and pray,
to listen in silence for Jesus,
and He tells me to be
as unexceptional as dust,

as clear and simple as water.

Francis Mourns His Father

Father, you labored against the high men
who would slight you and toiled
to raise me beyond yourself—me
with my habits flagrant with purple
and fur, good looks and gold—until
the nods you received deepened to bows.

Yet, your heart was only as large
as a fat purse and it paid dearly for me!
Every one of my swords and banquets,
each cape's precise cut, caps by
the dozen, the crow of young cocks
under your windows at midnight.

But wrong in your rich way,
you hated my love of poverty,
damning my salvation. I remember
that day I stood for the first time
a poor man in a line of beggars,
just another dirty face only
Christ would recognize!

Someone offered me a crust of bread
and we ate by the roadside happy
and ignored, as all the world's
business poured past. Oh, yes,
I confess! I confess! I came home
over my head in prayer and my body,
like a bandit made off with my thoughts.
I confess: I sold your finest horse
and all your cloth of gold to give
to the church—I who was not yet
alive to the vagaries of evil
or simple enough to sense
the utter simplicity of good.

But, father, you robbed yourself blind
bringing me up on charges before the Bishop.
When I gave you back everything, even
my clothes, and stood naked before you
and Assisi, I took my new Father,
and would remember only
my mother, one of the blessed poor,
though sorely bruised, her cheek's
blue rim, part of your rising
darkness, father, I had to escape.

The Priest Who Doled Out Penance Only to Those Who Could Pay

Ask for an egg, Brother, and I'd give you
a stone in those days, yes, even though I was
a priest—the priest who doled out penance
only to those who could pay and pay well.
I, Sylvester, never sacrificed myself,
though I served at God's table.

I knew Francis then only by reputation,
as a little poor man walking straightway
out of this world on his bare feet—
a foolish forsaker of fortunes—
and I was all too willing to dash in
and grab what he willingly dropped.

The day Francis joined Brother Bernard
to help him give away all he had
to the poor, and—believe me—he had
a great deal. I let Francis know my mind:
how he had begged stones of me for far less
than fair value and now that I saw him with
a fortune at his disposal, I let him know
I felt more than a little cheated.

He told me what I expected to hear:
that he *had nothing then and nothing now*,
but then he turned and filled my hands
without counting, gold and silver in such
a stream that my hands could not hold it.
A small fortune fell at my feet
and I with it on hands and knees to retrieve
every last coin. I did not even thank him,
but hurried off less I be asked to give any back.

That's how I was and would be even now,
but Francis—at that moment, he became
the measure of my mean and aging life.
I could not shake his smile, his open hands,
the savor of God's presence.

What could I do? I began to give alms
and when everything was gone, I joined him.

Sparrow Study

Francis calls others to join him

Perhaps you've found like I did
that you're never more hungry
than when satiated by food, more thirsty
than after those long nights measured in cups.

Perhaps you've shaken the long fever
of youth and felt your slack purse, its last
coin spent. Perhaps you already know
the stranger in the face of friends,

their walk away rudeness, whispers
from their lips like small quick knives,
and you've sunk, bruised and skinned,
a clutch of bones only Christ could love.

Come then and walk with me in His Way.
Enjoy feasts of turnips and leeks, and sleep
well under our blankets of leaves.
Friends, come study the sparrows

so common and brown, the trees silent
and still, their meditations heavy with fruit.
Come learn with us to pray, to rise
after midnight, to stand and wait

through the long passage of dark.
O, dear friends: To know our Lord's
infinite yearning! His love makes us sing
from the depths of our longing!

How Francis Gave Away the New Testament

When the mother of two Brothers came for alms,
Francis asked: *Do we have some for our mother?*

For he honored any mother of his brothers
as the mother of them all. After a search

which turned up nothing, but their New Testament,
the one they read their lessons from each day,

Francis asked them what it told them to do.
"It says to sell all we have and give to the poor."

So give it to her that she may sell it for her needs.
But when he saw their dismay and confusion

that he would give away what seemed to them
their one holy necessity, he touched his brow

and asked: *Brothers, isn't it already here?*
And then his heart: a*nd here?*

On Sweeping the Temple

Yes, he often carried a broom and swept
the dirt and refuse from ill-kept churches,
but I did not understand why until
that night I felt myself failing from
too little food and too many penances.

My heart weak, my breathing shallow,
I felt the dark press in to smother me
and I bolted up, dizzy with panic
and cried out like a giddy fool:
"I'm dying! Help me! Help me! I'm dying!"

A voice called for a lamp and then blessed
Francis asked *Who said, "I'm dying?"*
Ashamed I confessed it was me.
What's the matter? he whispered, *Why
are you dying?* "Of hunger. I'm dying of hunger!"
I blurted, abashed, and braced for his rebuke,
but he surprised me and all my sleepy
brothers for he smiled and called for a table
to be set so we could all eat together.

When we had finished, we sat silent
before the dawn of another day,
and he spoke to us with quiet firmness:

*Brothers, we all need to bring our bodies
under control or we will be more than
dangerous to one another, but we must
also provide them with what they need.
Our Lord desires mercy more than sacrifice.
Too many of you have beaten yourselves
with hatred, rather than swept and ordered
and loved yourselves as God's temple.*

The One Who Thought Nothing of Money

Yes, I am that Brother, the one who
touched the little coin, held it up
to the light, shined it on my tunic;
the one who mindlessly fingered it
and then tossed it on the window sill.

You think the penance he gave extreme,
perhaps mean, even downright cruel:
to kneel in the road with the coin
in my lips and thrust it in dung,

but I was the one who thought nothing of
money one way or the other, who could
thoughtlessly play with it and hold it
or let it go, who had no judgment.

It was only with my knees in the dust
that I saw my world, a little dung heap
and in the heart of it, placed by my own
soiled lips, the coin. It was then that I rose
and smiled and said: "Brothers, this I did gladly."

Another Use for Donkey Dung

Why I said what I said that day I can't
remember, except that that brother had
done me no wrong and even the presence
of others didn't dampen me. Like flint,
my hardness sparked a tender of irritations,
my temper flamed and fed my blazing tongue.

I threw hot words like stones, *hard*, stones
meant to wound deep and scar. And I knew
I'd found my mark for I saw his gaze drop,
his shoulders fall slack, and he turned half
away in pain. I could scarcely have done
more damage as David with his sling.

My heart that seized on him seized now
on me and suddenly sick of myself,
I dropped to my knees before him and took
the only sure cure: a chew of manure.
Yes, friends, donkey dung remains
my best of stays against my poison tongue.

The Tiniest Portion

Call this our place of pure beginning,
St. Mary's of the Little Portion,
hardly any portion at all!
Just big enough to hold
a few brothers at prayer.

Our Portiuncula,
built in ancient times,
deserted, dilapidated,
and filled with debris,
until Francis swept
and repaired it.

These tiny cells of wattle,
they're ours. Stone and mortar's
forbidden. Our food's whatever's given,
often not much, but when you're
hungry, anything tastes good!
We go barefoot, the poorer
our clothes the better,
worn and patched,
cinched with rope.

"Spare us!" hisses the World
"and spare yourselves,
for so many have so much
and Holy Mother Church
stands great with gold and
whores and jeweled power."

But we will be what we are,
men and women of little need
and no desires of consequence,
who make themselves nothing,

but servants to all: barely
a taste of God's kingdom,
the tiniest portion,
given for you.

Dancing before Cardinals

> *"...when he spoke the words*
> *with his mouth, he moved his*
> *feet as though he were dancing...."*
> — St. Francis of Assisi
> *Thomas of Celano*

I beg but the time your fingers
drum on the table, a meager
hearing at best, for my head's
a poor pavilion.

I'm God's idiot, can hardly
see the scratch on the skin
of the page, or read it out loud—
breath heavy, ragged, throat sore,
the taste of blood in my mouth.
I can't even grasp simple things.
My spoon slips into the soup.
I cup my hands and wait for rain.
I step out of the boat and sink
so Christ can save me.

Fathers, you know these are cold times,
you who receive all with gloved hands.
Naked under your thick robes, you
shiver, knowing the nature of sheep,
how they ramble and stray, their noses
to earth, eyes only for grass;
how they crop and rip it out
by the roots, leaving the meadow
brown with the scars of close grazing.

Fathers, forgive if I gather
words as I go, if when I speak
I can't help moving my feet,

for I do not carry the grave
and terrible weight of the church,
like you, you who must the shrewd
beyond evil. My poor tortoise
of thought makes its slow round and turns
up little. Yet, I bring no lies
or compromise, no wealthy trade
of words, Fathers, no caravan
of chatter to be ambushed by
Silence.

You see the truth of me,
Fathers, small like my Friars, those
little brown sparrows of men.
God counts them over and over.
He gave them a home in the air,
their food and their feathers.
They've no pride, just the pleasure
of wings, their dip and glide and slip
on the rippling wind. They're simple
by nature, Fathers. We who aren't
must be simple by grace.

Not Without Witnesses

> *"After I had been at the Curia for a while,
> I encountered a great deal that was repugnant to me."*
> — Jacques de Vitry, Reformer
>   and Bishop-Elect of Acre, 1216

No. I didn't use that word lightly.
Rome's become *repugnant* to the faithful:
a city of ruins and tombs, thieves
on their knees, and beggars, their
desperate hands like unanswered prayers;
its empty Basilicas, each a cavern
silent under its high roof except
for a few murmuring shadows
and the shuffle of slow feet.
The air's dense with the drift of dust
and sanctuary lamps gutter out
in God's unheeded presence.

And the Curia, most of the Papal Court,
have grown heavy and gross with the world's work—
with the buying and selling of benefices,
lawsuits and litigation, rulers and kingdoms—
They measure all words by their effect
and few ever speak of the Truth.

But take heart, my friend.
Even now in this last time, God's
not left Himself without witnesses.
You may find them like I did
if you lose yourself giving alms.
His new men, though beggars,
are quite unlike the rest.
They need little, seek even less,
and share most of what they're given.

You'll know them when you meet them:
men with no sandals or slippers, clothing
so worn and patched it's no more than rags
and tatters with a frayed rope at the waist.
And if you ask them who they are, they'll say
God's fools, little brothers, little poor men,
men by the sun baked brown like bread,
their hands rough as pumice, but light
and gentle in their touch as vellum;
hands given to living the gospel in prayer
and the care of lepers and the poor.

Cabbage Planting Made Simple

Cabbage Planting Made Simple

We two had come to see Father Francis
and ask if he would receive us as Brothers,
but we found him busy with the harvest.

He shouldered a basket of freshly picked heads
to the garden, set them down, and regarded them
for several moments, then eyed us likewise.

Let us see how well you plant cabbages.
As you see me doing, sons, you must do.
And he dug a hole, chose the fattest head,

thrust it in upside down and covered it
all but the roots. Yes, and so he went down
the whole row, heads down, roots up, all the way!

My poor partner looked at me with more than
panic in his eyes, even as I took a cabbage,
dug my hole, and pushed it in head first.

Good! Father Francis smiled and returned to his
own planting as I proceeded with mine.
My companion could stand us no longer

and shouted the obvious: "Father! Brother!
You're putting them in upside down!" Francis
simply replied without looking up, *Son,*

I want you to do as I do, but the man
could not bear such foolishness and refused,
so Father Francis said to him, *Brother,*

I see that you are a very learned man,
but go your way—you will not do
for my Order. Then our Francis

turned to me and grinned: *Now, brother,*
let us be cabbage heads and pass through
the world planting everything upside down.

Sparrow Seed

I came to Francis often and again
to beg for a Psalter, hoping to wear
him into permission: "It will help me
in my praises and prayers," I claimed, my heart
hard set for the thing. Brother Francis, knowing this,
turned to the fire's edge, scooped up a handful
of ashes and sprinkled them upon his own head.
This is my Psalter; let it be yours now too.

Yes, he stood against our keeping of books—
not against books, mind you, but their keeping!
Have only a few suited to poor brothers,
he said, and what do we Brothers need
but a little sparrow seed.

Sparrow Feathers

I still wanted a Psalter for myself.
I could read, though not very well,
so I sought it like the persistent widow
in scripture, though I do not mean to say
our Brother Francis was an unjust judge.

He'd already told me months before:
*After you have a Psalter, you will want
a breviary and after you have it,
you will want a fancy chair, ordering
 your brother to bring you your breviary!*

He was not, as some thought, against learning,
but the *vain* desire for learning. He knew
how it often led to pride and how pride
will wander into the welter of ideas
that leads to brain fevers and death.

He knew me far better than myself, though
I was new among the brothers, a novice,
and I confess now that I was reluctant
to resign myself and persistent in my pride.
Told *no*, I would go away, chagrined,

only to have my desire insinuate itself
to nag once more for his permission
even though he was often weary and ill.
He even began to call me, *Brother Psalter*.
I bowed, "That's what again I humbly ask

to have and to hold," and to my astonishment
he said, *Go and do as your minister tells you.*
I smiled and turned to go back the same road
knowing my minister would grant what I wanted.
But Francis stood still in the road, turning over

what he'd granted: *Wait, brother! Come back.*
He knelt and confessed he was wrong to say yes,
and turned my heart completely to our work.
The more we brothers take for our journey,
the more we veil what we were called to be.

A sparrow should take nothing but his feathers.

Francis Proposes to the Lady Clare

> *I [Francis] resolve and promise for myself
> and for my brothers always to have the same
> loving care and solicitude for you as I have
> for them.*
> — The Form of Life of Clare of Assisi

I give you my hand, its scars,
these bare feet with their blessing of dust,
and our Lord's love filled with fools.

I promise you the beauty of a man
shorn of swagger and brag, love's
essential poverty, its ragged sheep.

I give you water's cleansing kiss
and the only Son you will ever bear
as we spend this night, two

candles burning in a rude church.

Clare by Name and Nature

> *"...bright in life and
> brightest in character."*

I am Agnes, Little Sister to my
Lady Clare. Yes, we were sisters first,
and then more than sisters, Christ's brides
and wives and no one else's. *Poor Clares*
all call us now, though we're richer in our
simple poverty than ever in our wealth.

We were the first to come to Father Francis,
simple girls who did not realize great
families do not give their daughters up
without a fight. They raised us for alliances,
marriages of fortunes. We were treasured,
not for ourselves, but to be dickered with,
paid out on promise of reciprocity.

So when Clare stole away to Father Francis,
they came for her with torches and swords,
some drunk and all burned to black anger
and smoldering wrath, enough to kick in
the chapel doors. First they advanced
with flattering promises, then lisping advice,
but when those had failed, they moved to frighten her
by force with much banging of blades against stone
and fists against wood, screaming profanities
to cow her into submission—
but she would not be cowed.

She locked arm to altar, bared her tonsured head
and stated *No way will I be torn from Christ's service!*
in a voice so level and steady, it snatched
away both their breath and their resolve. They were

reduced to futile siege, for she was a fortress
that would not to be taken

But when I joined my sister, they deemed me
for some dim reason one loss to God too many
and came to take me back with harder words
and threats than used on her. They saw it
as their vengeance, punched and kicked me
unconscious before Clare's very eyes.
One uncle even yanked back his mailed fist
to give a lethal blow, but tore his muscle
and yelped in pain. They made to drag me
by my hair through the brambles and thorns
down the mountain, but they staggered to a stop
and set me down, not having counted on carrying
God's own dead weight in me. Clare caught up
with them, catching them up with such words
of shame that they ran away like guilty boys.

Other women soon joined us and we became
a Sisterhood with Clare our mother,
though when we sought to name her
Abbess, she stoutly declined, declaring
it a cross she was not called to bear.
Poor Clare! She had not counted on being
compelled by Brother Francis to accept.

Even then she rarely gave an order.
She preferred to do things herself rather
than order others and so she waited tables
like the rest of us, washed the filth and stench
from sickbed mattresses, and even bathed
and kissed our hands and feet. She knelt once
to give such a kiss to one who would not
tolerate such humility and kicked her.
Clare calmly took the foot again
and, on its sole, firmly placed her kiss.

Some say she was made clear by Christ,
but she would say He only made her Clare.
Some say she understood Francis more simply
and correctly than anyone else, but that's
hardly true as he well knew who often
corrected her and gentled her harsh nature.

Her Sisters, who didn't know she heard, whispered
her the woman even popes found they couldn't soften,
though those Holy Fathers had the wisdom not to try
when faced with Christ's own will.

She would say little for herself except,
Christ only made me more stubborn than most.

Francis Speaks to His Daughters

We had called and called for Francis, begged
even the Holy Father to intercede with him
and command him to come to us,
for we loved to hear and see him.
His very presence fortified our faith
and if we had our way, we would
have kept him with us always.

We loved him more than a father, more than
a brother—in truth even more than our Lord,
the way too often of men and women for one
another—but he would have none of it,
knowing the danger we put us all in.

When he came to us, we could see he was
not pleased and when we had assembled,
he raised his eyes to heaven in silent prayer.
Then he stooped for ashes and sprinkled a circle
around himself and dusted his head with them.
He stood and recited Psalm Fifty:

> *Hear, O my people, and I will speak,*
> *O Israel, I will testify against you.*
> *I am God, your God....*
> *Mark this, then, you who forget God,*
> *Those who bring thanksgiving*
> *As their sacrifice honor me;*
> *To those who go the right way*
> *I will show the salvation of God*

He said nothing more—ashes he was,
surrounded by ashes. He simply fled
from us without another word

and we wept, ashamed of ourselves.

The Day the Door-Gate Fell Upon Our Sister Clare

No. It was no ordinary door, but
the very door-gate to our convent,
heavy oak with iron hinges and studded
with reinforcing nails. It took four or five
of Father Francis' Brothers to hang it
and it did good service for many years,
such good service no one noticed the hinges
working loose from their settings in the wall
until the day our Mother Clare tugged its
handle and it slammed straight down upon her
like the massive wall of Jericho.

We called without answer and, frantic to lift it,
for we feared her dead, found our poor weak hands
could get no purchase on the thing in spite of our tears
and shrieks for help. Finally enough townsmen
gathered to lift it, but only at considerable strain
to themselves, barely able to return it
upstanding, we bracing ourselves for
the sight of her crushed and bloody body—

but there she lay, un-bruised, un-battered,
staring up at us, as surprised to see
our tears as we were to find her alive.
She told us she felt no weight to the door
as she lay there as in her grave. It seemed
like Heaven's Gate and all she had to do
was wait in faithful patience and it would
be lifted up to her salvation.

Gubbio Cheese Cake

You have heard of Gubbio's wolf,
but let me tell you of its cheese cake.

A woman, her face a veil of misery,
of sadness, lived there, her hands

useless fists of curled fingers,
swollen joints, blue and bruised.

She held them out to Francis
and asked him to touch them,

and he did, drawing those fingers
open, once more slender and supple.

At home again, in joy, she made cheese cake
with those hands and offered it to Francis.

He smiled and blessed her and took a little
and bid her eat the rest with her family.

Saint John the Simple

Aye. He was simple, not simple like Francis,
but simple like simple, and we treated him so.

He plodded behind the plow like an ox,
slow and heavy, and thought like an ox,

hard, head down, neck in the yoke and back
to the switch. Like all of us, he wanted

to serve the Lord, but unlike us,
he simply did not know how.

When Brother Francis said, *Give whatever
you have to the poor,* John said, "Let me give

this ox, what I deserve of all my father's goods,"
which put his poor parents in tears at losing it.

Francis bid them, *Be easy. Be easy.
I only want your John to be my brother.*

But soon we noticed when Brother Francis
coughed, John coughed. When Francis raised

his hands in prayer, so did Brother John,
and when Francis spat, John spat.

We blushed at his stupidity
and sniggered behind his back.

Finally even Francis was compelled to ask:
Brother, why do you do everything I do?

And poor John quivered, "Brother, omitting
anything's dangerous, when you're simple."

Francis, graced with simple kindness, said:
It is enough you follow me in prayer

and giving alms and charity to all,
and from that day, he became

for Francis: *Our brother, our Saint John.*

Whenever Asked for Prayer

We were making dusty time along a road
when a horseman approached and Brother
Francis recognized a precious friend,
an abbot who had great love for him.

The good Father dismounted and they
folded into themselves by the roadside
and spoke of the soul's salvation well
into the afternoon, until they entered

a long deep silence—a silence,
which the abbot finally broke
with his simple "Pray for me."
And Francis with his *I will gladly.*

I rose and we returned to our journey
but for a short distance, when Francis said,
*Brother, wait for me a little while again.
I want to pray for our friend, the abbot.*

And so we turned aside once more
for whenever asked for prayer,
he would offer it as soon
as possible, lest he forget.

The Hungriest Thieving Murderers

Even thieves get hungry, even killers suffer,
and we were the hungriest thieving murderers
to prowl the country round Monte Casale.

It'd been a bad winter and little came our way
to take, for the roads were empty of well shod
citizens. We'd become bone without meat,
weak enough in hunger's haze and fatigue
to beg—and to show you how desperate
we were, we actually went to the Brothers.

We'd heard of their kindness, even to lepers,
and we reasoned we were simply lepers
of another sort, for what other than
leprous hearts would do what we did.
We'd heard of their kindness, but
the Gate Keeper would help none of us
and gave us what he felt were our deserts,
whether just or unjust, a flail of bitter words
and stinking accusations that sent us
away darker, more ugly, than we'd come.
If he'd been outside the gate and if we'd
the strength, we'd have made short work of him!

But Father Francis, when he heard the Brother's
proud report of thieves sent packing, would own
none of it and sent him, as penance, packing
after us with provisions and a promise.

We hadn't gone far and were easy to find.
We'd laid low by the side of the road, hoping
against hope for a fat bird in our snare
when, lo, what's this! The same rough brother
comes stepping along with a wine jug
and sack of bread and—before we could rush him—
he kneels in the road and ever so humbly asks

our forgiveness. But what really gutted
our bloodlust, he asks us for Francis to do
no more evil and, if we agree, Francis
and the Brothers will provide for us.

We had to turn that one over in our minds.
Cagey men like us hadn't survived so long
without weighing and reweighing every
proposal, plot, and possibility.
Could such as us be forgiven? Made good?
We had no hope, being maggots preying
on the living, dead men good only for pike
or dungeon, or a dagger in a drunken brawl.

"What are you called, Brother?"
"Angelo."
"Angelo, eh? Tell your Francis, 'Thanks, but....' "
I couldn't say it: the "no" to slam the door
on that whimsical tag end of hope
floating like a rose petal between us.

He simply bowed and blessed us and was gone
and we settled in to finish our minor feast
and ruminate the offer. Evil sore
pressed in upon us and we knew
Death's Angel sought us everyday. Yes.
We could feel the Devil's scorched breath
on our backs and hear his minions lisp and spit
our names every time we laid our fire.

So, by solemn vote, we three decided
to seek this Francis out and try his promise,
and to our mild surprise he received us kindly
and pledged to seek our forgiveness.
Thus we joined his Brothers and I these fifteen years,
the last of the three still alive, continue
to tell our story: how he brought us to God,
not by cruel rebukes, but by sweetness.

# We Are to Walk Gently

We Are to Walk Gently

Aye, our Brother Francis, he delighted
in speaking to birds. He spoke to us, didn't he!
Every sparrow and crow, plover and pigeon,
and all of the swallows, every feather
of us flocking together to hear him.

When we came into the garden again,
he gave us instruction: how, if we needed
wood, we shouldn't cut down the whole tree,
so that it might bloom again, and when we set
to with shovel and hoe, we should leave

a border for the greening grass and set
aside a little place for sweet smelling
flowering plants. If we trod on stones,
even though they be sharp and cut us,
we were to walk gently as men of the Rock,

and lift worms from the road lest they be trod on,
though some mocked us in their wormlike way.
And in the winter, we were to set out
our best wines and honey for the bees,
so they would not perish from the cold.

And if we fell blind and fire was brought
to heal us, we should simply say: "Be kind
to me, Brother Flame; be courteous, for
I have loved you greatly in the past. Lord,
may I bear it, when you gently burn me.

Francis and the Rabbit

A Brother found the little rabbit snared
and exhausted and near shock, its body
beginning to stiffen in the cool evening.

He gathered it up and held it close
and it began to revive in the warmth
of his tunic, so he carried it to Francis,

Francis who murmured, "Brother rabbit,
why did you allow yourself to be
deceived so? Come. Come to me."

Our brother released it and it fled to Francis
who received it with pity's gentle hands
and it lay quiet against his bosom.

Francis smiled and caressed it
with a mother's affection and then
released it so it could go free to the woods,

but it returned time and again to his hands
until he commanded it be carried
by his Brothers to the nearby woods

and bid it be again at home there.

Francis Insults God and His Feathers

Yes, yes, yes! Brother Francis preached
to the birds, but, friend, the birds!
They didn't always listen!

Oh, no. I don't deny the time
he spoke to that great congregation
of crows and doves and daws.
Crows, mind you: they can be hard
to preach to, raucous and given
to picking things apart. And doves!
As restless a flock of feathers
as one can find! But Francis stepped
among them preaching, and even
when his robe swayed and brushed their heads
and backs, they did not start or squawk,
and flew only when he blessed them.

But this time when he saw a field full
and bid us wait while he turned aside
and addressed them, they took wing,
swooped passed him with angry chitter
and chirp, flashed feathers and vanished.

As Francis returned to us, we heard
how shaken he was, upbraiding
himself in the worst curse he knew:
*You impudent son of Pietro
Bernardone! You impudent son!*
And when we asked him why,
he confessed he'd taken on himself
too much, thinking his way with the
creatures was his and not God's.

How the Poor Point Out Your House

> At Bologna, Francis rebukes his Brothers
> for owning property and drives even the
> sick among them into the street.

I, who called you in the beginning,
called you with these simple words!

*Brothers, if you will be perfect,
give all you have, deny yourselves,
take up your cross and follow Christ.
God's politeness puts things simply.
Courtesy demands we simply obey.*

You say I brought you nothing
but the intimate baptism of dew,
Sister Rain who knows everything,
given time. You say you need
books and buildings and better beds,
our Rule softened and refined with gold.

Brothers, your compromises are mice
that will nibble and breed until the grain's
gone. Your barn resounds with the squeaks
and quibbles of small mouths.

See how the poor point out your house,
its stone and mortar, your elegant robes,
your books with their tooled leather.
They mark how your voices simmer
against the light and they hiss: "See!
See what his brothers have become!"

I call you to leave this place no later
than now! I would rather have you naked
and sick in the streets like myself,
than wallowing here.

Because the House Is Ours, Not Yours

I saw our Brother Francis angry, not
once, but often, after he returned from
his journey to Jerusalem.

Our rule was clear—"houses only of wood
and wattle, hovel small and humble"—but
he found us building a kingdom of hardness,
like that place in Bologna, all stone
and fine woods, rooms filled with books,
a house of study, a hospital for our sick:
a place we thought he could not speak against.
It was a palace people came to point to—
how we had risen so fast and far to *this*—
but Francis would have none of it and ordered
even the sick, to flee in haste, like Lot
from Gomorrah, without looking back.

And when he returned to Assisi that year
for our annual Chapter, he found
the city expected such a multitude,
hundreds and thousands of Brothers, and it
had built a great stone house to hold them.
Brothers, he cried, *we must tear this down!*
as he climbed to the roof and sent a cascade
of slates and tiles crashing to the ground,
but a knight shouted: "No, Brother! This isn't right!"
And Francis, surprised that anyone would
so oppose his order, said: *And why not?!*
"Because the house is ours, not yours."

Oh, he said. *Oh.* And he came humbly down.

Saint Fraud

Remember that Brother who joined us
for a time, like some very poor pilgrim?
How he seemed the very body and soul
of holiness, outwardly outstanding,
prayer itself! He kept the holy silence
with such strictness that he never spoke
with words, preferring only signs.

Yes. When he sat among us to hear
good words or scripture, how
he appeared so graced with joy
he moved us all by his devotion
and we whispered him a "saint,"
and would have brought him to Brother
Francis' notice when he came to us—

but when Francis came he would have
none of him, deeming him deceitful
and a fraud! Even our Servant Minister,
Brother Elias, was shocked and chided Francis
for rejecting such holiness, "a pureness,
Brother, that *only you* will not accept."
Others chafed at Francis and whispered
that he suffered from more than blindness
if he couldn't see the obvious: a purity
that drew us as Christ's must have drawn
his disciples.   A few even murmured "envy."

But Francis wouldn't swerve and simply said,
Order him to confession and you will see.
Elias hesitated, ill at ease, but finally did so,
and none of us rose to protest it, knowing
that command was sound and true.

We stood confident of vindication
only to see our man, whose every gesture
we had graced with significance,
put his finger to his lips and shake
his head with such defiance it was clear
he would not, by any means, confess.

We stared, stunned and silent,
for the first time uncertain what he was
and when he looked to us, we looked away.

His once sunlit face waned in days to twilight
and when he knelt to pray he soon left his knees,
restless with impatience. He stood mute
and less than moved as we sang the Hours,
and soon disappeared from among us—

and now he's out there somewhere,
as close and coy a counterfeit as one
might find, trolling again for fools like us,
all too easily seduced by rapture's first blush.

When I Grew Tired of Walking Behind My Brother

I walked, he rode, and nothing seemed right,
not the sun's heat on our backs nor the marsh
with its clouds of gnats and mosquitoes.

Follow in our Lord's footsteps, he often said,
so we went barefoot and patched together,
hungry and shunned more often than not.

"Follow in our Lord's footsteps," I murmured
as I stewed in my sweat and irritation,
my sole duty to plod behind his mule,

quick stepping now to avoid its droppings.
I, who had given up so much—station, lands,
and fortune—far, far more than *him*.

He slumped on the beast, as if ill at ease,
oblivious it seemed to all around him—
and I was so occupied with myself,

I didn't see him stop and dismount and near
stumbled into him. *Brother,* he said, *it's
not right for you to walk and me to ride,*

for in the world you were greater than me.
More than a little ashamed of myself,
I sank to my knees and confessed

my thoughts in tears, as I do again now.

Francis Explains What It Means to Be Bound and Led in Truth

You think me extreme to have a Brother
lead me through the streets with a rope

around my neck and shout my sins
and failures to the people? Then

you understand neither sin nor me, sin
that slithers in by little sideways slips

nor me who never works by inches.
Brothers, we must not deceive ourselves

or others about ourselves. You only
know me truly when you know how

the first time I ate among the poor
I made sure it wasn't in Assisi.

Even when I begged oil to light the lamps
at Saint Damian's church I feared to be

seen by my former companions and shunned
lepers until Christ would have none of it.

I found the discipline of silence
and work as difficult as anyone,

for my hands were soft from easy gestures.
My sins are why I've never been one

to walk the middle mild and gentle way,
and am never one to hear the devil out,

his soft, sonorous recommended compromise.
We must slay him with a single stroke, Brothers,

and only be bound to one another in truth.

# That Winter of His Faithfulness

That Winter of His Faithfulness

We went uncommonly by horseback that day,
an order of the bishop, Brother Francis
weakened by fevers and much in pain,
our bodies whipped by sleet and rain.

I drove my horse against the gale, breathless
for shelter and warmth until I realized
Francis had faded far behind and stood
beside his horse, head bowed against the rain.

I cursed my hard pace then, fearing I'd caused
his horse to falter or, worse, him to fall.
But no. When I drew close, I saw his lips
moving and knew what the matter was.

When he journeyed through the world on foot,
he always stopped to say the hours. Illness
and hard travel changed nothing for him
and he'd gone to ground in time for prayer.

So, together we chanted that long hour
in the gray wash of waning afternoon.
He shivered. I shivered.
Our horses quivered the gathering snow

from their backs, but stood steadfast and solid.
We remembered the long patience of God
and when we finally remounted
he murmured more to himself than to me:

Praise God who is faithful in all weathers.

How We Lost Our Mantles

We labored along that winter,
the cold severe and Francis not
well, the way so hard that for once
he wore a mantle, one of two
good ones lent us by a friend. I
wore mine with great thankfulness.

A crone, either shrewd or sly
who felt she was poor and in need,
must have sized up our dear brother
as a more than easy mark and begged
him warmth against the terrible cold.

To her great surprise and mine,
and before I could even whisper,
"Brother Francis, that's not ours
to give," he shifted his mantle
to her shoulders and smiled:
Go. Make yourself a dress
which you greatly need.

And without so much as a "bless
you, Brother!" She was gone, lest
she be asked to give it back.
I could see by his pallor
how the cold cost him,

but he'd have none of my mantle
claiming I'd be the poorer for it—
at least until she came again,
having found his cloth fell short
of what she wanted. He turned
to me and tapped my mantle:
For the love of God, Brother.

I muttered "For the love of God,
Brother," and lost my warmth
as she took it without question.
And when she was gone again,
this time for good, and we stood
shivering in the driven sleet
he murmured not so much to me
as to himself: *Not only the coat
but the cloak, Brother. It's not
always easy, not always easy.*

Why Francis Begged Meat and Ate Grapes in the Vineyard

He who was by then the most ill
took very little thought for himself,
but much for others.

When people sent him choice morsels
from their kitchens to strengthen him,
he passed them to those among his

brothers who were sick, especially
those tossed about by temptations
and near to fainting in spirit.

He ate on fast days so the ill
should not be ashamed to eat
and he would even beg meat

in the market for sick brothers,
though some whispered a *true* holy
man would not eat so high.

Yes, I've seen him do these things,
I, who was ill and cared for by
his very hand—yes, me,

the sick brother with a longing
for grapes and ashamed of it.
He led me into the vineyard

and ate first to give me courage
and then we made a small feast
of it, and when we had finished,

he begged me not to become angry
or disturbed in illness against God
or my brothers. *Bear your troubles*

patiently and give thanks for them,
he said. *Don't let a sheep be lost
for want of patience and kindness.*

The Man with Murder's Face

No one willingly approached me, no,
not with alms or questions or compassion,
not me, the man with murder's face,
hatred's eyes, the glare that warned
"I will kill you if you cross me."

None, that is, but Father Francis, though he
who'd known me once, hardly knew me now,
and nearly passed me by. He saw only my rags
at first, the face and body beaten by
more than weather. Then he spotted something
familiar, someone he'd known in the world,
and so he asked *How are you, brother?*

I couldn't raise his eyes to meet his gaze,
let alone return his joy. I winced at
the gentleness in his touch and stopped, stark
still, to draw the heaviest of breaths.
"I'm bad off, very bad off, thanks to my lord,
God damn him and all of his to hell."

That had been my only prayer for months
even though by damning him, I damned myself,
and Francis knew it and would not have it so.
Brother, set your soul free: forgive your lord.

But I couldn't. He'd treated me worse than his
dog which at least had gristle and bone to chew.
He'd kicked me in the heart, took my house
and all my crops, shamed me before my wife
and family, and barred me from his lands.
He'd sent me alone into winter's white teeth,
hoping they would savage and silence me.
Francis listened and thought. Both of us shivered

from the frost, but I the more for my rags. *Here.*
I'll give you my cloak and beg you once more
to forgive your lord for the love of God.

It was the smallest of gifts against the world's
great cold, but he had given me all he had
and then I fell into his arms and wept
and then I could forgive.

On the Proper Use of the Fox Fur

We argued only once and that over fox fur,
a small skin, hardly enough for a pair
of good gloves, but I, as his appointed
guardian, thought it might be of some use.

He wobbled along, hobbled by pain,
his stomach unsettled, his spleen enlarged,
deep winter's raw bitterness whipping
his threadbare tunic. He shivered at times
so hard he could not speak, but simply stood,
back to the wind, and hugged himself till
the worst of the gusts abated.

I wanted the fur sewn inside his tunic,
but he would have none of it, so I argued:
"If not the whole, at least some to cover
your stomach and give you some relief!"
After all, half a pelt was better than none.

Then not inside my tunic, but outside,
his voice hoarse with pain and the weather.
I heard, but could not agree: outside
would have less effect, perhaps none at all!
And so we went back and forth until
he saw I was losing all patience, laid
a calming hand on my arm, and said:
*Inside out. Inside out. I must not appear
differently outside than I am within.*

The Morning Francis
Taught Us All to Sing

Portiuncula, 1224

Jerusalem was in the past and Rome.
He would try only a few more local travels,
these on his Brothers' arms, their voices his eyes.
His stomach, spleen, and legs were weak,
but it was his eyes that failed completely.

Sister Pain proved his constant companion,
so much so that sleep abandoned him for weeks.
He could not abide the sun by day
nor his beloved firelight by night.
Only darkness gave relief so we lay

him in a hut's dim corner, a cell covered
with mats, but then another visitation
befell him: a plague of mice. His hut's
walls and roof thatch crawled with them,
the Devil sent temptation!

So bold and busy they were, they scrambled
over and around him even as he sought
to sleep and nibbled each meal he tried to eat.
Yes, we tried to trap them, but they were
too small and fast for our slow hands,

and he would not allow us to send them
harshly to their deaths. Time and again
we heard him murmur, *Dear Lord, Dear Christ,*
make haste to help me bear all this with patience.
and many of us stole quietly away

in tears for none could comfort him.
We feared that Sister Death could not be
far behind he suffered so. So! Imagine
our surprise when he called us to him
and not for last farewells. He asked two

of us to write and all to learn by heart
as he composed. His voice, first low and hoarse,
grew stronger with each word until he was
singing, and we were singing too, the first
to sing his *Praises of Our Brother Sun.*

Francis and the Body's Poverty

In those last days, Brother Francis bore quietly
all the most difficult gifts of Lady Poverty.
He hid his pierced and shattered hands
within his sleeves, lest anyone see
their truth, but his face told its own story:
gray with pain, temples red seared from
cauterizing irons; eyes swollen and pasted
shut with salves—our failed attempt to save
his sight. When he rose to walk, he limped
at best and favored his right side, the side
where his tunic often bloomed with blood.
If it were not for his smile, his gift of peace,
people might have turned from him in horror.

On the morning his legs failed him completely
and he knew he would never stand again,
Francis sat and prayed in silence for a time,
then with a mischievous smile called four
Brothers to him and designated them
his "four new columns for his failing house."
From that day on, they carried him.
When he bled, they cleaned and dressed
his wounds and they whispered in his ears
all that was before them, so he could see.

Many sought to know their names, but modesty
allowed them only the four Francis
gave when he chose them: *Brothers Patience
and Simplicity. Brother Discretion.
And the most robust: Brother Gentleness.*

The Little Dog Speaks of the Blind Man

"Yes, brother, I was his guardian
in those last few years before his death."

Why I was picked I do not know except
that Father Francis begged of our new
Servant General, Peter of Catania,
a guardian who he could cherish
as his superior. I've always felt
a novice, as poor a brother
in obedience as one could be, but
Father Francis rejoiced in my selection
and said: *Fear not, Little Brother
I, too, am a novice before Christ
and would obey a novice of even one hour
just as carefully as the oldest brother.*

God forgive me, I was hardly comforted
by this, for I've seen that with most men
it is one thing to hold the reins and quite
another to be directed by them.
He who knows high office rarely steps
down with grace, let alone humility!
Seeing how thoroughly unconvinced
and nervous I was, given my new office,
Go with me, he said, *from place to place
only as the Lord inspires you,* and then
he put me at my ease, when he laughed
and whispered only for me to hear,
*I once saw a blind man with a little dog
as his guide along the way!*

Father Francis proved more than a lesson
in poverty and chastity. He was

the very soul of perfect obedience.
His was not submission in resignation,
but joy. I couldn't have been his guardian
if I hadn't seen that, how he spoke to the
Brothers in the Great Chapter that elected
Father Peter to succeed him, saying:
*From now on I am dead to you, but see,
here is Brother Peter whom I and all
of you shall obey*, and though we wept
and would not have it so, he, in his
increasing infirmities, confessed he was
unable to give us the care he knew
we needed and in prayer commended
the whole family of us to our Lord.
He bowed low, did reverence to Brother
Peter, and took the lowest seat in Chapter.

That he did not give his burden for us away,
but continued to carry us in his heart,
came clear to me one of his last autumns
as we sat with our backs against an early frost
and warmed ourselves at the fire.
He gazed long into it with that special
contentment I have often seen,
but finally he sighed and bowed
under some unseen burden.

"What troubles you, Father?" I asked.
He drew his fingers through the dust
and ash on the ground before answering:
*That there is hardly a religious
in the whole world that obeys perfectly.*
I followed that in my simple ignorance.
"Tell me, Father, what's perfect obedience?"

And to my surprise, he spoke of corpses:
When men are dead, do they resist being

moved? Murmur over their position?
If set in chairs, they look down, not up.

But when he saw my confusion, he smiled:
And are we not dead to the world, little
Brother? Should we ask why we are moved?
Care where we are placed? If raised up, shouldn't
we be the same humble dust we've always been?
And then he paused, but after a moment added:

And shouldn't we look twice as pale in purple?

Poverty Clothed by Christ's Mercy

We all knew his time was near to leave us
and he most of all. And he knew that to be
a faithful lesson to us, he must own
nothing when he died and return to God
as he had come, so he commanded:
Place me naked on the naked earth.

And though his brothers did not fully
understand what he was trying to say,
they obeyed in autumn's cooling twilight
and stripped and lay him shivering on the clay.

But though they were well familiar with his
blindness and how his legs had failed him,
none knew, and only saw then, how
gravely wounded and broken his body
was, the gash in his side which he tried
to cover with raw and bleeding hands,
his feet twisted, useless, and blue.
Some gasped and many wept and all stood
helpless as he lay suffering before them.

But I could not be still as his guardian,
and moved by my Lord, I knelt and began
to cloth him, speaking loud for all to hear:
"I command you under holy obedience,
Brother Francis, to accept these clothes
I lend you for now and, so that you may know
they in no way belong to you, I take away
all your authority to give them to anyone else!"

The others stared, quite stunned and shocked
that I would speak thus to our holy Father
and treat his wishes so, but he, himself, smiled

*Brother Guardian, you have clothed me
with Christ's mercy. Free now from all,*
he whispered to our Lord, *I'm coming to you free.*

A Note on the Author

Terry H.S. Wallace is Emeritus Senior Professor of English and Creative Writing. He is an editor, publisher, and the author of ten books, including three of poetry (*Beyond the Neat Houses Cheap Talk Built* (1988), *Raw on the Bars of Longing* (1994), *When the World's Foundation Shifts* (1998)). He is also extensively published in both scholarly periodicals and literary journals (including *Cumberland Poetry Review, The Sewanee Review, Poet Lore, Christianity and Literature),* and anthologies (including *Odd Angles of Heaven: Contemporary Poetry by People of Faith* [Harold Shaw] and *Identity Lessons: Contemporary Writing about Learning to Be American* [Penguin]). He lives in Camp Hill, Pennsylvania, with his wife, Diane, and his daughter, Emily Elizabeth Xinyu.

www.ingramcontent.com/pod-product-compliance
Lightning Source LLC
Chambersburg PA
CBHW031205090426
42736CB00009B/790